Copyright 2018 by Stewart O

All rights reserved. No part of
distributed or transmitted in a
photocopying, recording, or o
without the prior written permission of the copyright holder, except in the
case of brief quotations embodied in critical reviews and certain other
non-commercial uses permitted by copyright laws.

First Edition

Dedication

This book is dedicated to my deceased maternal grandmother, Ellen Stewart, who introduced me and my brother, Charles Joseph Odendhal III, to the Unitarian Church at an early age.

To Chris,
Stay happy & healthy
Stew Odendhl

Table of Contents

Introduction **5**

Chapter one

Select a church **8**

Chapter two

A miracle **10**

Chapter three

A prayer answered **12**

Chapter four

Confusion in a Catholic Church **15**

Chapter five

Dogma or reason **19**

Chapter six

A missionary's mission **23**

Chapter seven

A movie that moved me **28**

Chapter eight

Books to ponder **29**

Chapter nine

You are a Hindu, right? **31**

Chapter ten

The many gods of India **33**

Chapter eleven
Kids are taught to Lie **35**

Chapter twelve
Is the cow in India really holy? **38**

Chapter thirteen
What you see can hurt you **42**

Chapter fourteen
Like father, like son **44**

Chapter fifteen
He's not my brother and she's
not my sister **47**

Chapter sixteen
Mormons think; do you think? **49**

Chapter seventeen
It depends upon what you know **51**

Chapter eighteen
Whose belief are you going to believe? **54**

Chapter nineteen
A little twig will do ya **56**

Chapter twenty
You have to hand it to some religions **57**

Chapter twenty-one
What is the difference between science and religion? **58**

Chapter twenty-two
What happens to Muslim women when they die? **60**

Chapter twenty-three

Discussion and summary **61**

Conclusions **75**

References **77**

Acknowledgements **81**

About the author **82**

Introduction

Never ever be afraid of saying, to yourself or anyone around you, "I just do not know." It is nothing to be embarrassed about. How else will you ever be motivated to learn? Besides, no one ever knows everything. As the twentieth century humorist Will Rogers said, "Everybody is ignorant, just on different subjects." (Carter 1991).

I am motivated to write this book because, in my ninetieth decade of roaming around the earth, I am amused and perplexed about how so many religious people casually mention the oxymoronic statement "religious truths". In many cases nothing could be further from the truth. If every average 8th grader in school is properly educated, he or she should know: human births cannot take place without sexual intercourse or *in vitro* fertilization; humans cannot walk on water; humans cannot arise from the dead; one cannot turn swords into plowshares; and the sun cannot stand still. To teach such fantastic farfetched farcical falsehoods as truth constitutes child abuse as Richard Dawkins has said (Dawkins 2006). Last year when I told that to one of my very best friends, he responded, "Child abuse, hell. It's adult abuse as well."

Ultimately, I don't know, you don't know, we don't know, they don't know, and nobody knows for sure whether there is a god or not. Religious scholars may claim that there is a god, but they cannot supply rational verifiable evidence to substantiate such a statement (Budziszewski 2003). The secular atheist claims that there is no god, but he or she cannot show any ironclad convincing argument to back up their statement as well (Navabi 2014). So, for lack of proof, each group appears ridiculous to be so insistent on their position when adequate means to do so, does not exist. The most truthful statement is that neither side is capable of proving their side, or disproving the other side. In other words, the question of, "Is there a god, or no god?" is very obviously not knowable.

The question that disturbs me the most is how some religious people can believe things that are virtually impossible for school children to comprehend and difficult for them to believe in, and yet they are capable of physically attacking those who challenge their beliefs even when some aspects are obviously unknowable. A recent Nobel laureate, Daniel Kahneman, provided a partial answer to this question when he wrote in one of his books, "We know that people can maintain an unshakeable faith in any proposition, however absurd, when they are sustained by a community of like-minded believers." (Kahneman 2011).

It is instructive to note that true fundamentalist believers of one god will not hesitate to kill those other religious believers who believe in another god or who do not believe in any god at all. So the take home message here is that arguing about religious matters with true believers may sometimes be hazardous to your health. Atheist and agnostics on the other hand, have no axe to grind and usually do not attack or kill those who do believe in god (Dalton 2015).

I feel uncomfortable using simplistic labels to describe or refer to human characterizations or personalities. It is almost impossible to capture the essence of anybody or anything by a single descriptive term. However, if I had to refer to my current personal religious awareness, I would say that I am a happy self-content inquisitive slightly atheistic agnostic. I will explain in more detail this designation later in the book

This book is chronologically arranged in chapters, each of which describes a critical observation or anecdote during my journey from religion to reason and self-discovery. The initial chapters involve my early life and educational periods. Many of the later chapters involve episodes described from the pages of my daily diary that I have habitually maintained during my research activities which have taken me to many different parts of the world (Alaska, Australia, Bangladesh, China, Denmark, Eastern Europe, France, Haiti, Greenland, Hong Kong, Iceland, India, Italy, Kenya, Mexico, Morocco, Norway, Sweden, Switzerland, Thailand, United Kingdom and several Caribbean islands).

The last chapter deals with an amalgamation of the individual critical observations, other experiences and how they all interrelate to each other. Toward the end of this chapter, comments are offered on the comparison of religion and science in general terms and various experiences of cross cultural misunderstandings.

Why should I bother to write this book? It appears to me that we are all, to a certain extent, prisoners of our own culture; unfortunately that includes religion. While for many people religion brings comfort and security, for others they feel constrained and entrapped by rigid codes and creeds of such a controlling nature that it destroys their feeling of freedom. Apostates of Christianity (Andrews 2013, Barber 2012, Williams 2014), Judaism (Kneale 2014) and Islam (Rizvi 2016, Warraq 2003) have recently come out of the closet, so to speak, and described the refreshing invigoration of their lives by becoming atheists or agnostics. I therefore wish to act as a catalyst to give courage to those who wish to escape the smothering distorted nature of religious control.

So, please do yourself a big favor; honestly ask yourself the following question: What would you believe about birth, life, death, and god if you were me after experiencing the significant sequential series of critical observations described in this personal journey of enlightenment? As one of my mother's best friends told me when I was 21 years old, "If you are worried about dying; you ain't living!" Why on earth concern yourself about unanswerable questions when no one has a clue (du Sautoy 2016)? Accept these wondrous mysteries as they are. Forget about the past and the future; just enjoy the now and make the best of it (Tolle 2005).

Chapter 1

Select a church.

Shortly following the end of World War II my mother met and married a returning Army Air Corps service man in Oklahoma City, Oklahoma. This ambitious individual, who was a lawyer (and will remain nameless for many reasons), sought (I suspect) to join the church with the largest number of wealthy and influential members. His ultimate goal was to get elected to the Oklahoma State legislature and pursue a career in politics. Toward this suspected goal, the whole family (myself, my older brother, my mother and stepfather) began attending a different church every Sunday for a number of months.

We went mainly to the Anglican (high Episcopalian), Presbyterian, lower Episcopalian, Methodist, Lutheran, Church of Christ, Baptists, and a few others that I cannot remember. My stepfather finally decided that the family should join the Anglican (high Episcopal) church downtown. I was around 10 or 11 years old at that time and was directed to go sit with the boys who would be attending the religious education classes during the main services. Unfortunately, I sat in the wrong pew and ended up in the second year class of religious instruction. Therefore, I was slightly smaller than the other boys and had to defend myself during class time and on the playground. As a consequence, being highly spirited, I managed to get into trouble now and then.

It was difficult for me to concentrate during the religious education classes in Sunday school because the older kids pestered me and I returned the action in kind. One Sunday the topic was the Jewish celebration of Passover. I found the instruction of some interest, but did not pay a great deal of attention.

The following Sunday, in Sunday school the teacher started out saying that we would review what we allegedly learned last week. The teacher called on various students to answer some of his questions during the start of the class. Eventually, my turn arrived and he said, "Odend'hal what was the animal of the Passover?"

I slowly repeated his question out loud; stalling so that my brain could search for the answer which could not be found. I sort of recollected that when that topic came up last week that I heard what sounded like the word "bird" and associated with that word was another word that resembled "duh". Putting the two words together, I blurted out, "Bird dog".

The class came unglued and they could not stop laughing. Some even pounded the tables in jubilee of such a ridiculous response. The teacher was not happy. Trying to control his anger he slowly said, "The animal of the Passover was the dove. And speaking of which you Mr. Odend'hal can act like a bird and fly out of this room this minute and wait for your parents outside until the end of the services."

As I walked out of the door, I heard him tell the class, "He's such a nice kid. I don't know why he is so disruptive."

My maternal grandmother, during the same time frame, took me with her to the Unitarian church one Sunday. Again, I was sent off to a religious education class. But here I was placed in the correct age group. However, this time the instruction seemed much more logical to me. The teachers explained things so that the stories seemed to make more sense. As an example, at the Baptist church, the teacher would say that Jonah was swallowed up by a whale and God came to save him and took him from out of the whale's stomach. In contrast, the Unitarian teacher would say, that Jonah might have passed close to the whale's mouth, but was not actually swallowed. Further, she explained in a lucid manner, that some of the other Biblical stories may have been exaggerated for effect, or parts of the explanation may have been lost in translation. In other words, the Unitarians gave us little kids some credit for having brains, whereas the Baptist teachers told us stories that just did not make sense and appeared divorced from reality.

Chapter 2

A miracle.

When I was 12 years old I wanted a dog and my mother and stepfather after numerous arguments finally broke down and bought me a young German shepherd. I named him Sarge. He had been with the family only about a week or so when he just disappeared one day. For two or three days we looked all over for him to no avail.

During that next weekend, I was determined to find him and spent all morning walking the neighborhood and going farther away from our house, calling his name and looking everywhere. Then, almost around noon, I walked by a Baptist Church (they are everywhere in Oklahoma City) and in desperation, I prayed with all of my heart to God (the only one that I knew about at that time in my life) to help me find my dog. Like a miracle, about 15 minutes later, I saw him trotting along the sidewalk across the street from where I was. I called him. He stopped, looked at me and came bounding across the street into my arms.

I was so enamored with my successful communication with God and His help, that I decided that I was going to become a preacher when I grew up. To that end, I directed brief religious family services after dinner every night for about two weeks. At each service, I assigned Biblical readings to different members of the family, and I said a prayer and picked out study lessons for everyone for the next day. The family was cooperative, but not terribly enthusiastic. In the end, sports trumped God and after dinner I played baseball with my neighborhood buddies.

I appreciate the saying that, "God helps those who help themselves". Therefore, I also believe in the power of an individual's sustained effort to reach one's intended goals. If you want something bad enough and are willing to work diligently toward that goal with all of your heart and soul, chances are you will be successful. So, later on, I suspect that will power and persistence were more important than God's help in finding my dog. Another thing that may have crossed my mind at the time may have been the following. It may have seemed to me that there were other people in the United States and, indeed the world, that had much more pressing and urgent problems that God should have attended to which should have been a higher priority.

Chapter 3

A prayer answered.

When I was 14 years old, I played right half-back on my Junior high school's football team. In the last football game of my life, I took a hand-off and was just about to score a touchdown when in my peripheral vision, I caught the sight of Mickey Fentress bearing down on me from the side. He was a tough line-backer and weighed about twice as much as I did. He hit me squarely and very hard so that as I landed on the turf, my right knee hit the ground first.

My right knee did not like that and went haywire, i.e. I consequently suffered what is known as a lateral luxation of the right patella. That is, my knee cap was displaced out of the joint and rested very tightly on the outside of the joint (where it did not belong), locking my leg in a frozen 90 degree angle that caused excruciating pain. I could not straighten my leg and neither could anyone else.

What followed was a flurry of activity, with much hollering and everybody telling everybody else what to do. Eventually, a stretcher was found, a station wagon was allowed to drive on to the football field and I was transported to the closest medical doctor in the area. This doctor was well meaning, but apparently had never seen a luxated patella before.

Because my leg was frozen at a 90 degree angle, they were unable to carry me through the door into the examining room. So they put me down on the floor of the waiting room and with all of the patients (4) gathered around me the doctor said, "Sometimes they go back into place." He was referring to the right knee cap that had gone haywire.

With his strategic decision announced, he tried to push the knee cap back into the proper location of the joint. This accomplished nothing, but caused additional excruciating pain. His next statement made much more sense, when he said with some reluctance, "Perhaps it might be better if we called an ambulance and had him transported to Mercy Hospital."

The pain never subsided. The ambulance came, but unfortunately the route to the hospital, approximately 10 miles away, included a segment of road construction where the road bed had been completely torn up. So there was one sharp bump, or ditch after another. This particular leg (pun intended) of the trip stretched for only approximately a half mile. But it seemed like a mini-eternity. The ambulance driver was sympathetic and was aware of my pain, but slow as he would go, the pain was unrelenting and I was miserable.

About half way through this construction area, silently I prayed with all of my heart and soul for God to make my pain go away. And, lo and behold, as soon as I said that, my pain subsided and gradually disappeared. What I felt instead of pain, was a gentle tug on the attachments of my knee cap with every bump; but no longer was the pain intolerable. With the relief of pain, I was very grateful to God.

When we got to the hospital outside of the emergency room, the ambulance driver opened the door of the ambulance and went to get a gurney. As I lay in the stretcher an attractive young nurse stuck her head into the ambulance and in a very cheery voice said, "What have we here?"

I responded that I had torn my knee out from the joint.

She patted my affected leg which reignited substantial pain and said. "Don't worry about anything. They will just remove your knee cap and you'll have a stiff leg for the rest of your life. But everything will be okay."

As I recall, I did not believe her because she was so good looking that I didn't think that she needed to be smart.

I was eventually sedated and the knee cap was replaced in the proper location of the joint and I wore a cast for about three months. When the orthopedic surgeon finally removed my cast, I could hardy bare any weight as my muscle mass in my right leg had under gone disuse atrophy and was much smaller than my left leg. The doctor's last statement as I hobbled out the door was, "Don't come back to see me until you can do 100 knee bends."

So, I never came back to see him. To this day (67 years later) I have never been able to do 100 knee bends.

With regards to my belief at the time that God had answered my prayer, much later I learned in veterinary school that under extremely stressful circumstances, involving tremendous pain, the brain releases endorphins which have the power and action to reduce pain. So, in retrospect, I no longer attribute the reduction of my pain to some god given power of some holy entity to take the time to single me out from millions of others suffering pain to fix my particular situation.

Chapter 4

Confusion in a Catholic church.

One summer, when I was 15 years old, my uncle paid me 25 cents an hour to work in the freight yard of his lumber company unloading box cars of lumber, roof shingles, sacks of cement, and other materials. It was back breaking labor and the heat was severe. One day after work at home my 19 year old brother, Charles, asked me "Hey Stew, do you want to go to Rhode Island and meet our biological father? I am taking off to go there next week."

"Gosh Charles, I had no idea that you were planning to go there. Of course, I want to go there with you."

Unlike my brother, I was too young when our parents were divorced and I had no recollection of our biological father at all. It was as if I had never been with him before. However, I admired him very much for his exploits and heroism during his naval career in the Second World War.

While I was excited about going, I wondered where we would get the money to go there. Charles told me he had received two hundred dollars from our great grandmother for the trip. Then, I voiced a major concern about the proposed adventure; "I hope that mother will give me permission to go."

Charles answered immediately in his usual big brother smug attitude, "Don't worry about that. We can handle it."

Our mother and alcoholic stepfather were on vacation in Colorado at the time. They were due to call us that evening. Sure enough, the phone rang at the appointed time and we had a pleasant discussion about our respective geographical areas and the weather. Then the sensitive topic of travel to Rhode Island was broached.

The conversation, emotions, hysterics, hollering and anger that followed could probably fill half of the Sunday, New York Times magazine. Their reaction was that I could not go and if we persisted with this idea, then Charles could not go. So, we reacted like any other "normal" teenagers, i.e. when Charles slammed the telephone down, we looked at each other for a second or two and both said at the same time, "Let's go."

Then, we essentially stole the family car and took off for Rhode Island almost immediately. We drove the back roads, so as to avoid the Oklahoma Highway Patrol, which we just "knew" would be after us. We each had armed ourselves with two peanut butter and jelly sandwiches and a thermos of apple cider. We kept listening on the radio to see if the cops were after us.

We reached St. Louis, Missouri around mid-night and got lost near the Budweiser brewery where there was a tangled web of narrow streets and dark alleyways which I found frightening. Once across the Mississippi River I went to sleep in the back seat and Charles continued to drive. Around 2:00 am I woke up and saw that Charles had pulled off of the highway on a dirt road and was snoring away. I felt scared and asked Charles if I could drive so he could get some rest and sleep in the back seat. Even though I had never driven before and did not have a license, he agreed. I was so anxious to get back on the highway that I had not taken the time to find out which direction we had been headed. So, after driving for about an hour I saw a road sign that said, "St. Louis 21 miles". I never told Charles about my error.

In Baltimore we tried to meet our fraternal grandparents but a neighbor told us that they were vacationing in Atlantic City. Baltimore was like a foreign country to me with all of the row houses that I had never seen before. Eventually we arrived in Fort Adams at the entrance to the Narragansett Bay near Newport, Rhode Island where our father lived.

Meeting my father was one of the high lights of my life. He was non-authoritative, not an alcoholic, had a good sense of humor, was caring and just a super nice guy. His wife, my stepmother, was the mirror image of my stepfather. It was like out of the frying pan and into the fire. She was an alcoholic, pernicious, capricious and a Catholic. So, every Sunday the whole family, including my four half-sisters, my brother and I, were commanded by her to attend the Catholic Church in Newport.

I will never forget that first Sunday. We walked into the Catholic Church and in the foyer, there was a basin on the wall filled with water. Like everyone else, I dipped my finger into the water and flipped some of it on to my head. So far, so good, I remember silently saying to myself because I had emulated the veteran attendees successfully. That turned out to be beginners luck.

We got into a pew and I was suddenly transported into a different world. All of a sudden, everybody stood up and so I followed suit and stood up, only to find just as suddenly, I was the only one still standing and everyone else was now sitting. So, I sat down, and just as suddenly, everybody was standing again. This awkward non-rhythmic uncoordinated exercise continued throughout the entire service and I repeatedly was standing alone with everyone looking at me and wondering, 'Where did that retard come from?'

The parishioners mumbled words I could not understand at various times. At one point, it sounded like they were saying, 'I can play dominos better than you can.' Then, the sermon was in a foreign language that was, well, Greek to me. I later learned that the entire sermon was in Latin; which was the only course that I subsequently flunked in high school.

After church at home I complained to my Dad about the fact that I did not know what to do and did not understand a word of the service. He was sympathetic, but insisted that I try again next Sunday with an open mind, since I now had the initial experience under my belt. To accommodate his wish, I did, but the same thing happened again and I felt like a fish out of water.

So, the following Sunday as everyone was getting dressed to go to church I said, "Really Dad, I just do not want to go to church this morning. Last week was just like the week before and I get nothing out of going. I don't understand what they are saying. My movements are uncoordinated with everyone else and it is just not fun. Would you mind if I did not go today? I would much rather play tennis."

To my utter surprise, he answered, "Okay, if that is how you feel, you do not have to go to church anymore." Thus, endeth my Catholic Church attendance for life.

Uh, oh, I have to correct the inaccuracy of that last sentence. When I was 17 or 18 years old, I spent a weekend at Lake Murray Lodge in Southern

Oklahoma with a Catholic friend of mine. We got drunk that Saturday night and caroused around until early Sunday morning. We did not have a hangover because we were still on a high and rip roaring drunk with no sleep at all.

My friend told me that he had to go to church. I thought he was kidding, but he insisted that he could not miss attending church. That was because he would have to undergo some sort of penitence, like saying 100 "hail Marys" or some such falderal. We negotiated the steps of the church amazingly well, but staggered down the aisle before collapsing into a pew giggling. I only took communion to prevent my friend from falling down (which luckily he barely avoided).

I wondered at the time, how a religion could be so intimidating that their devotees would risk such embarrassing behavior to save them for having to confess or do some other corrective activity. Then, I recalled that I had heard that the Catholics had a saying which stated, "Give me a child until he is 12 years old and he is mine forever more."

In those days in Newport, Catholics could not eat meat on Fridays. So every Friday we had fish. I tried to understand why that was, but the real reason was never explained to me satisfactorily. Years later, some mortal or mortals decided that they would stop having the sermons in Latin and rescind the need to eat only fish on Fridays. I still wonder to this day, how those changes were decided and by whom.

Chapter 5

Dogma or reason.

I attended a parochial high school (Episcopal) and then went to the University of the South, in Sewanee, Tennessee, which was also Episcopal. At both places, daily attendance of a chapel service was mandatory. I, of course, memorized the usual litany of the creeds and songs and knew the Bible fairly well, even though my Sunday school attendance had been irregular earlier. I never thought much about the deeper meaning of these indoctrinations, but sort of went along with the crowd and enjoyed the time spent at both academic institutions.

My junior year of college, I transferred to the University of California at Los Angeles (UCLA). I was freed from the obligatory daily chapel scene. On rare occasions, I did attend the first Unitarian Church in Los Angeles and enjoyed the thoughtful and stimulating sermons delivered there.

I was dating a girl from Pasadena, and she invited me to attend Christmas Eve service at the Episcopal Church in Pasadena. Being familiar with the routine, I took communion with the rest of the attendees. However, when I returned to our pew with nothing to do while the rest of the congregation took communion, I began to read the common prayer book at random.

At one point, I began reading the Apostles' Creed, which I had memorized years before. The Apostles ' Creed states:

I believe in God, the Father almighty,

Creator of heaven and earth.

I believe in Jesus Christ, God's only son, our Lord,

Who was conceived by the Holy Ghost,

Born of the Virgin Mary,

suffered under Pontius Pilate,

was crucified, dead, and buried;

He descended to the dead.

On the third day, he arose again;

He ascended into heaven,

and sitteth near the right hand of God, the Father,

and he will come to judge the quick and the dead.

I believe in the Holy Ghost,

the holy Catholic Church,

the communion of saints,

the forgiveness of sins,

the resurrection of the body

and life everlasting. Amen

As I read it, it suddenly dawned upon me that I really did not believe any of the statements which it contained. It was even a revelation to me that at one time I had joined in unison to chant such obviously unrealistic, impossible, and contrived statements.

Next, I turned the pages to the Nicene Creed which states:

I believe in one God,

the Father almighty,

maker of heaven and earth,

of all things visible and invisible.

I believe in one Lord Jesus Christ,

the only begotten son of God,

born of the Father before all ages,

God from God, Light from Light,

true God from true God,

begotten, not made, consubstantial with the Father;
through him all things were made.
For us men and for our salvation,
He came down from heaven,
and by the Holy Spirit was incarnate of the Virgin Mary,
and became man.
For our sake he was crucified under Pontius Pilate,
He suffered death and was buried,
and rose again on the third day
in accordance with the Scriptures.
He ascended into heaven,
and is seated at the right hand of the Father.
He will come again in glory
to judge the living and the dead
and his kingdom will have no end.
I believe in the Holy Spirit, the Lord, the giver of life,
who proceeds from the Father and the Son,
who with the Father and the Son is adored and glorified,
who has spoken through the prophets.
I believe in one, holy, catholic and apostolic Church.
I confess one Baptism for the forgiveness of sins,
And look forward to the resurrection of the dead
And the life of the world to come. Amen.

I also rejected the Nicene Creed also, as it too must have been contrived. Up until that time, I had always answered the written questions about my religion, as Christian. But for the first time, I thought, perhaps I should not claim myself as a Christian anymore as that would constitute hypocrisy. However, I still believed in a higher power and assumed that there was a god.

Chapter 6

A missionary's mission.

Just before I graduated from UCLA in January of 1960, I had heard a very stimulating question, i.e. what was more beneficial to a person, four years in college or four years traveling around the world? Since I had just completed four years in college, I thought it might be interesting to have four years traveling around the world to answer that question for myself.

So I sold my car and bought a steam ship ticket which would take me from Los Angeles, across the Pacific Ocean, through the Suez Canal and the straights of Gibraltar and eventually to Southampton, United Kingdom. My third class ticket paid for my board and room expenses for two and a half months while I was on the ship. My last stop in Australia was Perth, where I jumped ship and began hitchhiking back to Sydney because I had met my first wife on the Sydney to Adelaide leg of the journey from Sydney to Perth.

In Perth I stayed a week with some friends. They showed me an advertisement in the local newspaper that read "Young man in truck desires traveling companion back to Brisbane". The young man had lost his business in Perth and was transporting the machinery for making cyclone fencing back to Brisbane. The truck was very old and did not look very road worthy. He had trouble convincing me that the truck could make it as far as Sydney. But the price was right (zero) and against my better judgement I agreed to be his traveling companion.

After two days of driving across a wash board dirt road in the Nullarbor Plain a surprising and disturbing event suddenly took place. Without warning the truck abruptly stopped and listed hard to the right.

"What was that?" I asked the driver called Eddie.

"Whatever it was mate; it's a bad sign because there goes our wheel bouncing up and down the road ahead of us."

The physical injury to the truck was not lethal, but very discouraging. The diagnosis was a broken right front stub-axle.

After placing all of the injured parts into a filthy dirty gunny sack, Eddie looked off to the east over the flat desert expanse of the Nullarbor plain and said more or less to himself slowly, "One of us is going to have to hitchhike into Adelaide (700 miles away) to get the spare parts and one of us is going to have to stay here with the truck."

Without any hesitation, I said "I don't know who is going to stay here with the truck, but I am the one who is going to hitchhike into Adelaide."

Eddie gave me 90 quid (Australian pounds) with instructions to buy some tucker (food) in the first town that I should come to and ask the proprietor of the shop to ask travelers headed west to drop it off to him while I was searching for the spare parts. Within 3 hours the first car that came by heading east picked me up and helped me secure the needed spare parts in Adelaide.

Hitchhiking back to the truck was not easy. At one location it was particularly difficult to catch a ride. That was in the town of Port Augusta, South Australia. It was difficult because it was the rainy season in the Nullarbor Plain and very few people were driving on the extensive dirt (muddy) roads west from Port Augusta.

After hours of trying to catch a ride, in desperation I went to a gas station (petrol pump station) to have a captive audience so to speak, in order to entice a traveler to give me a ride after relating my sad story. Most of the folks getting gasoline at the station were not going west. Finally, a large Chevrolet Suburban pulling a small cargo trailer drove into the gas station. Inside was a stern looking man, a stern looking woman and two very young stern looking (exceedingly well behaved) children. The car was almost completely full and I knew that there was no space for me in the seating area of the car. However, I noticed when the stern looking man opened the back door, there was a very small space in the back, like a cubby hole amongst the pile of supplies in the back.

Even though I looked like a swagman (bum) in my dirty full length leather coat, carrying a grungy filthy dirty gunny sack, in desperation I approached the stern looking man.

"Excuse me sir. May I ask, are you headed west?"

"Yep.", came the reply as he scrutinized me with a suspicious expression on his face.

"How far west are you going? I have a friend in the middle of the Nullarbor plain that is out there waiting for me to bring these spare parts that I am carrying in this gunny sack and I need to get there as soon as possible to save his sanity since I have been gone almost a week." I pleaded.

"We are only going out into the reserve to bring the light of the Lord to the poor dirty Abo (native Aboriginals) devils. As you can see, there is no room in our vehicle for anything or any person." he replied, as he turned abruptly to walk away from me.

Quickly, I stammered, "That's not far from where our truck broke down and I saw in the back of your Suburban that there is a small space where I could ride in the fetal position and I wouldn't be a bother to you."

He turned to face me and said, "We camp on the side of the road when we travel and have no extra bedding. So I am sorry but we cannot take you with us."

"I could sleep in the truck."

"Kids sleep in the truck."

"I am desperate to get to my mate, so I could sleep in the back of the truck." I countered.

He seemed to weaken in his resolve not to accept my plea, and said, "Look. I'd like to help you, but I am afraid we cannot take you."

Sensing a sympathetic opening, I continued, "If you are a missionary going to help out the Aboriginals, it might be good if you could have some compassion for one of your own kind, who is in a great deal of stress. I would be so quiet, your family would hardly know that I am there in the back."

With a slight pause and obvious sigh, he said, "Okay, but you will not be comfortable back there because it is a rough ride out there in the Nullarbor."

He never bothered to introduce me to the rest of his family. He just whispered to them as I got into the back of the Suburban and assumed the fetal position. Throughout the first day's journey, as I recall, there was not much talk or laughter in the front of the car as we drove along. When we stopped to eat something on the side of the road, he did introduce me to his family, but they distinctly were not friendly at all. They had their food, and I had mine and we sat apart.

After we had stopped for the night and they had set up their tent, the kids went to bed in the Suburban. Then he invited me over to the fire and he obviously wanted to talk with me alone. His wife had retreated into the tent for the night.

When I squatted down on my haunches near the fire, he had a concentrated stare with his eyes strongly focused directly into my eyes he said, "Have you been saved, brother?"

Somewhat mystified by his question at first and suspicious of exactly where this conversation might go, I responded with a smile on my face, "Well, I don't reckon I'll be saved until I get to my buddy's truck."

Without changing his expression he said, "No, have you been saved from eternal damnation in hell fire by taking Jesus Christ as your witness and savoir?"

I answered, "I really do not know what you are talking about."

He countered, "You see, if you do not pray with me now and pay careful attention to what I say to you, you will go to hell when you die."

"I don't want to hurt your feeling, but I really don't believe you." I responded.

"Listen to me here young man. This is serious business and I don't want to let you burn in hell fire. Jesus loves you and wants to help you. Take him as your Lord and master, or you will suffer dire consequences."

I said, "You mean to tell me that if I do not do as you say, Jesus will let me burn in hell fire?"

"I am sorry to say son; but, yes that is true."

"What kind of a loving Jesus is that? What about the pigmies in Africa that never heard of Jesus Christ? You are telling me that those innocent pigmies will burn in hell fire just because they never heard of Jesus?"

He responded, "Yes, that is true. And that is why I am going out to preach this vital message to the poor ignorant Abos in the Nullarbor Plain, so that they will not suffer when they die."

I just looked at him in consternation and said, "I'm tired. I think I'll go to bed now."

"You'll be sorry." He sort of whispered to himself as he headed toward the tent.

The next day, when we stopped to eat or go to a gas station, he approached me and asked me to reconsider and let him bare witness so I could be saved. I just politely said, no thanks each time and he eventually did not bring up the subject any more.

When they turned off of the main road (such as it was) in order to go to the reservation (as he called it), I got out of the car to continue hitchhiking west. I was so tempted to say, "I got into this car believing a little bit in Jesus Christ. But you have convinced me, because of your way of thinking, I will not believe in Jesus Christ any more. Your Jesus is a vengeful and uncompassionate god. Further, all you are going to do is probably preach sin to the Aboriginals and make them feel bad. Even though you claim that I am going to burn in hell fire after I die, I am pretty sure that I will not and I'll bet that we both end up in the same place." Unfortunately, I was young and had been taught to be polite. In retrospect, I wish that I had had the guts to say that to him at the time.

Chapter 7

A movie that moved me.

In 1963 a movie that I saw called "El Cid", had a strong impact on my religious beliefs at that time. In the movie about the battle for the control of Spain between the Islamic Moors and the Catholic Christians there were back to back scenes showing the leaders of the two competing religious armies.

In the first scene the leader of the Christians said, as his horse reared up and he raised his big sword, "In the name of God we shall kill those heathens."

In the very next scene the leader of the Moors said, as his horse hopped around, twisted and turned, "In the name of Allah we shall slaughter the infidels."

I had been taught at several different Sunday schools that the God of the Christians and the God of Muslims were one and the same. Both religions were from the house of Abraham and the only difference was that Christ was the prophet of Christians and Mohammad was the prophet of Allah (who was the same God, but just had a different name). Here (historically in the movie) the two religions were trying to kill each other in the name of the same god (as spoken through different prophets). Somehow the credibility of the respective combatants seemed to be at odds with one another. The use of religion as an excuse to kill each other seemed stupid to me.

Following this experience, I became more interested in the teachings of the Unitarian church. Detractors of Unitarians have said that Unitarians were: a non-prophet religion; prayed to whom it may concern; were atheists with children; was a philosophical society; and their symbol was a question mark that operated as a weather vane on top of their steeple and turned with the prevailing wind.

Chapter 8

Books to ponder.

On the ocean journey back to the United States from Australia during the early 1960s, one of the younger passengers was reading a big book with the provocative title of, *"Why I am not a Christian"*, by Bertrand Russell (Russell 1957). Back in Oklahoma where I was raised as a kid, most everyone would be horrified to see someone reading a book like that. If that person was a local resident, he or she would most likely be shunned and ostracized.

Having experienced a run-in with a fundamentalist Christian on the Nullarbor Plain, I was tempted to read the book. I asked the girl reading it if I could have a look at it. She said, "Sure." As I glancing through the book I thought to myself, 'Some avid Christian fundamentalist is going to kill this person.'

When I turned the pages of the book I remembered a book that my grandmother had given me when I was 17 years old. It was, *"Religion without Revelation"* by Julian Huxley (Huxley 1956). It had made a lot of sense to me then and this book by Bertrand Russell also seemed to make sense as well.

Afterward I bought and read, *"Why I am not a Christian"* and Bertrand Russell became one of my favorite philosophers. He was insightful, perceptive, clear and concise. It was obvious that his thoughts were based upon reality and not fairy tales that did not make any sense. Decades later I was so happy to see that books like, *"The God Delusion"* by Richard Dawkins (Dawkins 2006), *"The End of Faith"* by Sam Harris (Harris 2004), and *"God is not Great"* by Christopher Hitchens (Hitchens 2007) were all on the New York Times best seller list for many weeks.

In a recently published book entitled, *"Thinking Fast, and Slow"*, by the Nobel laureate, Daniel Kahneman, he succinctly revealed the real reason that religion survives in so many cultures today. On page 217, he stated, "We know that people can maintain an unshakeable faith in any proposition, however absurd, when they are sustained by a community of like-minded believers." (Kahneman 2011). I am well aware that this quote has already been presented in the Introduction, but it certainly bears repeating.

Chapter 9

You are a Hindu, right?

My junior year in the School of Veterinary Medicine at the University of California – Davis, I was seriously considering accepting a faculty position at Johns Hopkins University's School of Hygiene and Public Health which would involve living in India for two to three years. One day, I saw an announcement for a talk by a certain Hindu, swami Ananda Anandarandamanda (that was not his correct name, but close to it). He was scheduled to deliver a lecture at the Unitarian church in Sacramento on Hinduism the following weekend.

Since I knew that my job at Hopkins would entail living in India for a couple of years, I was very intent on learning everything that I could about India. I also knew Dr. Jain, a veterinary faculty member who was a Hindu and president of the India Association at Davis, California. Therefore, I invited him to join me to attend the talk. He agreed and we went together and we both enjoyed the lecture very much.

I had taken copious notes during the talk. There was a reception afterward, but rather than staying to try and talk about the lecture content with the swami, I offered to pay for Dr. Jain's lunch at Little Black Sambo's restaurant on the west side of Sacramento. While the choice of the restaurant was politically and culturally inappropriate to some at the time, the pancakes were delicious. Besides, I would have Dr. Jain as a captive audience and I intended to overwhelm him with further questions about Hinduism as we ate. As soon as we had ordered our yummy pancakes I took out my notes from the lecture and began to ask Dr. Jain questions.

"Dr. Jain, the swami said that Vishnu and Shiva were the same thing. How can that be?"

Following a pregnant pause, he replied somewhat reluctantly, "Well'um, I daun't know."

"Huh. Well, okay. Then, why is the monkey Hanuman so important?"

Another equally long pause ensued, "Well'um let me see. You know, actually, I hav' no idea."

All of my subsequent questions to Dr. Jain resulted in similar unknowing or vague responses. I eventually realized that any further interrogation would also most certainly result in the same embarrassing pause, with a subsequent denial of knowledge about his religious expertise.

To end the agony I said, "Gosh, Dr. Jain. You are a Hindu, right?"

He looked straight into my eyes and with a conspiratorial glint in his eyes said, "Well'um, let me tell you honestly. I think that Hinduism is mainly for little old ladies and children."

Chapter 10

The many gods of India.

During veterinary school in Davis, I sometimes attended the Unitarian church there. Unitarians were my preferred peers. Some were atheists, some were Christians, some were agnostics, some were Jewish, and some were ex-Hindus. What they all had in common was a great curiosity of the tenets and beliefs of other religions. I liked the agnostics the best because they had the courage to say, "I don't know."

Agnosticism appealed to me then and even now in my present circumstances for the following reasons. Theists and deists say there is a god. Atheists say that there is no god. Obviously, they both cannot be right. Therefore, one of them must be wrong as they cannot both be right. The argument to support their respective position, obviously is not supported by sufficient facts to convince the members of the other's position. Therefore, something just does not add up to a thinking person's standards of proof.

Once again I will state; I personally maintain that, you do not <u>KNOW</u>, I do not <u>KNOW</u>, we do not <u>KNOW</u>, they do not <u>KNOW</u>, and nobody <u>KNOWS</u> for sure whether there is a god or not. Therefore, why argue and kill each other based upon unknowable faulty reasoning. If you cannot prove something, let it go and turn your attention to something that is more worthwhile.

This brings me to the subject of religion in India. In the village where I lived on a daily basis for approximately two and a half years, the surrounding neighbors worshiped different gods with no animosity towards those who were different in their religious preference. One of my neighbors went regularly to the Shiva temple. Another neighbor prayed to Ganesh and another was a devotee of Vishnu. Then, there were those who prayed to Shitala, Lakshmi, and other gods.

The central fact was that not even one of the devotees ever had the arrogance, need or desire to change my religion to theirs. They were all comfortable with the god that they had. They never criticized the other gods; as clearly one's choice of a god was their own individual business and it was a very personal thing above reproach. The monotheistic religions should adopt the same mature attitude and the world would be in a much better and undoubtedly safer situation.

Chapter 11

Kids are taught to lie?

Eleven percent of the population in my study area in West Bengal, India were Muslims. The vast majority of the population were Hindus. During the house to house survey work to collect demographic data, after two years I could speak and understand Bengali (the local language) well enough that I was able to ask questions and record the answers in the questionnaire that we used. The Hindi language is different and it is the language of the more Northern provinces in India.

In the Hindu areas, my assistants and I were allowed to go to each individual household and conduct the interviews with the head of the household, or any of the adults (male or female) that lived in that particular household. In order to have a check on the initial survey, we returned to the same households and repeated the same questions every nine months. We repeated this check visit twice. This practice allowed us to confirm and validate the first survey and to determine the changes in the population and acquire more accurate demographic data. We also collected demographic data on all of the domestic and other animals in the individual households. Since the first and third surveys were exactly one year apart this allowed us to compute prevalence and incidence figures for various factors.

In the Muslim villages, we were not allowed to go house to house for our survey work for several reasons. When we entered the village, we never saw any women. They remained in the houses and out of sight. Therefore, we had to conduct our survey work at the mosque which (because they were poor villagers) consisted only of a concrete slab with no walls whatsoever.

The villagers would gather standing around us at the mosque (there were no chairs or tables) and we would take out the questionnaire from the previous visit and ask the same questions about the ages and sex of each person and all of the other animals in the household. If the farmer had more than one animal of the same species, we would always try to note some characteristic identifying feature of that animal, such as color, markings, scars, size, etc.

In this one Muslim village on the third (and last) visit, a remarkable occurrence took place. As was usual, almost all of the men (young and old) of the village would crowd around the spot where the interviewing was taking place. Because we were confined to the mosque, we could conduct only one interview at a time. My three Hindu assistants, remained next to me and let me do the interviews.

The head of one household had diligently answered my questions and I had completed the third survey. Then I took out the sheet that had the data from the second survey and asked questions about any differences between the last visit. At each previous visit to this particular household, there were three cows. However, one of the cows from the previous visit was missing and was replaced by a recently purchased cow. So, I asked the man, "What happened to the white female cow with the bent left horn?"

Before the head of the household could respond a small boy standing in the front row of the crowd very nearby, blurted out loud, clear, and proudly, "Amara kay-ye-chi." This statement clearly translated into English as simply, "We ate her."

Simultaneously, several of the adult men hollered out in Bengali, "No, no, he does not know what he is saying. No, no, that never happened."

As the consternation and protestations diminished and a brief uneasy silence invaded the atmosphere of the mosque, the little boy, with a very perplexed expression on his face looked around at all of the people who had contradicted him, and clearly stated in Bengali, "You all know that we ate her. Why is everybody saying that it is not true?"

I glanced momentarily at his father who I was interviewing. He was speechless. I quickly looked back to where the little boy had been standing in front of the crowd and he had completely vanished. I will never forget the surprise and look of indignation on the boy's face, as he tried to tell what he knew to be the truth.

Because of the reverence for cattle by Hindus, the Muslims are particularly sensitive to revealing any indiscretions or mistreatment of cattle. The

Hindus are aware of the fact that Muslims will eat beef, but as long as it is done out of their sight, it is acknowledged and tolerated. This is because the Muslims will buy and sell cattle and ultimately purchase the cattle that can no longer plow, work or give milk. The Muslims serve as an escape valve in order to salvage some value from the more useless older cows of Hindus.

The little boy who told the truth, undoubtedly, will learn to lie in the future if Hindus are around because of religious, ethnic, and cultural considerations.

Later after this particular incident I asked my three Hindu assistants what they thought of the exchange and did it bother them. They each said that while they wished that the cow had not been killed and had died a natural death, they realized that the practice did go on in Muslim villages and there was nothing that they could do to prevent it. They felt no animosity toward the villagers and they would not tell anyone about it.

I noted that in this instance, there were about 50 Muslims and only 3 Hindus and one foreign agnostic present. If the ratio was reversed and there were only 3 Muslims and 50 Hindus who were told that the Muslims had killed a cow, what might happen? They each acknowledged, that it might be highly probable that the Muslims would be severely beaten. (See the New York Times, Sunday, October 4, 2015 for: "Mob Attack, Fueled by Rumors of Cow Slaughter, Has Political Overtones in India.")

Chapter 12

Is the cow in India really holy?

When I graduated from veterinary school in 1967, I was immediately hired by Johns Hopkins University as an instructor in the Department of Pathobiology. The department had received a very competitive multi-year grant from the National Institute of Health, called Johns Hopkins University's International Center for Medical Research and Training. It was referred to at Hopkins as the CMRT in order to distinguish it from another international program at Hopkins. The CMRT was to concentrate on foreign diseases and other threatening conditions in India that would give American health professionals an exposure and experience with such infectious agents prior to their possible introduction into the United States.

The personnel studying in India were mainly physicians, but there were also, Ph.D.'s: parasitologists, anthropologists, entomologists, acarologists, statisticians, microbiologists, animal ethologists, ecologists, wildlife biologists, and one veterinarian (me).

My first month in Baltimore, I was invited to a dinner in Washington, D.C. to meet with the head of the Bombay Natural History Society. This delightful gentleman was a Muslim and he wanted to entice me to study and write a report on the idea that cattle were the main stumbling block that held back the agricultural development in India because of the Hindu's belief in the sanctity of cows. As that was the prevailing attitude throughout many Western scientific academic communities, I was not surprised, but I was reluctant to promise any total commitment to such an aim without further study on my part.

It is difficult to capsulize my trips to India (1967 to 1970; 1977 to 1978; 1981, and 1987). Grants that supported my work in India besides the National Institute of Health, were; the Ford Foundation (mainly in Bangladesh); the National Science Foundation, the National Geographic Society, the Indo-US Sub commission on Education and Culture; and two Fulbright Senior Research Fellowships.

In India I studied: the energetic ecology of cattle (Odend'hal 1972); transmission of foot and mouth disease virus by wildlife (Odend'hal 1979A; 1981B); Bovine Leukosis (Odend'hal 1982A; 1986); comparative milk production between foreign cross bred and native cattle (Odend'hal and Brown 1988); and the demography of humans and domesticated animals (Odend'hal 1980A and 1980B; 1988A and 1988B). With regard to the sanctity of Indian cattle, the journal Current Anthropology published several comments on that subject that the editors had requested (Odend'hal 1979B; 1981A; 1982A). With an individual grant from the National Academy of Sciences I did similar work in China from 1987 to 1990.

Space and time do not allow for a full in depth coverage of the issue of the holy cow of India. However, I will relate some of the major revealing facts.

First of all, it is deceptive and unfair to compare the practices of one culture to another culture based upon economic data alone. The value of the respective currencies changes on a daily basis. The infrastructure and mind set are often completely different. A much more logical comparison, should be on the basis of constructing an energetic balance sheet of inputs and outputs with consideration at the population level over a number of years. Unlike monetary evaluations which fluctuate on a daily basis, a kilocalorie maintains the same value and is stable over time.

When I calculated the feed consumption (input) and the human derived benefit (output) based upon the flow of energy (in kilocalories) for the cattle population in my study, it revealed that India cattle were more productive than American cattle; as only the affluent can afford inefficiency.

A key factor was the use of the dung that was produced by the cattle in India. Dung had many uses, one of which involved the use of dung cakes as a cooking fuel. As a substitute for coal, wood, or kerosene, (which were very expensive for the average villager), the dung cakes saved them substantial amounts of money.

All of the agricultural crops grown during the time I was there, were grown specifically for human consumption. None of the crops were grown to feed livestock. All of the cattle feed consisted of residues, such as rice straw and mustard oil cake which were derived from crops grown for human consumption.

If the villagers had used the rice straw directly as a cooking fuel, it would have been very inefficient. It would burn rapidly with an erratic uneven flame and the heat distribution would be very uneven and parts of the food might be incompletely cooked. In contrast, if the rice straw was first passed through the cow, it would not only supply the fuel for the cow's muscle power to do so many different chores, it would result in dung cakes. Dung cakes, which burn with a slow, even compact flame, are ideal for cooking.

The cattle at the village level in India, provide the power to plow their fields, take the produce to market, crush the sugar cane, produce milk, butter, cheese, and replacement animals, as well as the valuable cooking fuel.

The cow in India is the most essential animal for survival for the average villager. This animal plays a pivotal role similar to the horse for cowboys in the old American west. Cattle are so important that over centuries a sacred status developed. While outsiders look upon cows in India as holy, to the farmer it is a necessity. Even though a cow is a necessity, the head of a house hold will have no remorse to sell the animal, when he wants to get his daughter married and a dowry is required.

A popular portrayal of the holy cow in India to the western world is a picture of a skinny stray cow wondering throughout an urban area, with a caption that suggests these are useless cows. Many of such cows are owned and are turned loose in the mornings to have the cow go scrounge for themselves to eat any garbage they can find. These cows wander back to their owner's place in the evening.

As a matter of fact I was invited by Kumar (my driver) to go to his house in Calcutta for dinner once. He took me to the cow shed at the back of his house and showed me his beautiful strong milk cow that was well muscled and had a bright and shiny hair coat in the peak of condition. After a wonderful meal we walked around the neighborhood. As we turned a corner I saw an emaciated very thin cow walking down the street with ribs pressing against the tight skin.

Pointing to the derelict cow I said to Kumar, "Boy, there is a bag of bones, if I have ever seen one before."

Kumar replied calmly, "That's my cow."

"Sure it is and you probably own all of the other stay cows in the market too, right?"

"No, that's the only one I own." he said.

"My god, you are telling me the truth?" I responded.

"Yes, I am telling you the truth and you will soon see that the cow is on her way back to my house."

"Kumar, why on earth do you keep such a decrepit cow?"

"Well. You might not believe me, but last year she did get pregnant just wondering around the streets and I got a calf out of her. It costs me very little to keep her, as I just turn her out in the morning and she comes back in the evening. She is so unappealing that nobody would steal her."

There are no stray cows in the rural areas of India. They are all tethered along the roads and canals where they are periodically moved by their owners to new grazing grounds. The reason there are no stay cattle, is the fact that if someone turned their cow loose and it started to eat someone else's crop, they would be severely dealt with by the crop owner.

To sum up, only the affluent can afford inefficiency. The average villager in India must manage and regulate his resources for maximum benefit out of the necessity of survival. His cattle are a crucial resource for his production of food and commercial interactions. Through empirical experience he must be judicious, frugal and aware.

Chapter 13

What you see, can hurt you.

I was recognized throughout my study area in India because: A. I had a bright green Willis Jeep station wagon and very few people in the area had a car; B. I had white skin color that could be detected from a distance; and C. there were usually large numbers of little kids following me around everywhere (many of which would say loudly in very stilted English, "Whet es yor nam?").

One bright sunny day, as I was crossing a small bridge over a water canal that was choked with beautiful blue water hyacinth on the edge of a village, a Vaishnob (religious person) stopped to tell me about his sick cow. He was extremely intent and described the signs of the illness in minute detail. He was my same height and we were standing at the entrance of the small bridge, so that our shadows could easily be seen on the floor of the bridge foot path. Since it was late in the afternoon and the sun was low in the sky, our shadows stretched completely across the floor of the bridge from one side to the other.

While he and I exchanged a series of questions and answers about the health and history of the cow, I noticed a grandmotherly looking lady in a white sari (indicating that she was a widow) and a small girl standing behind the Vaishknob waiting patiently to walk across the bridge.

As our conversation continued, I could see the older woman began to fidget with her sari and was getting nervous. As the Vaishnob continued to talk, finally the woman seemed to well up all of her courage and she said in Bengali, "Please, Ba-Ba (father), would you mind walking to the other side?"

He turned around slowly and replied, "Oh. Yes, of course.", and we walked to the other side of the entrance to the bridge, so that our shadows were no longer an obstruction to her. Then she and the small girl walked calmly across the bridge.

Kumar, my driver, had observed this entire episode, as he was sitting in a tea stall nearby. After my conversation with the Vaishknob had ended and

I had agreed to stop by and examine his cow, I asked Kumar about what had taken place.

"What was that all about?" I asked him.

"Well, you see, the Vaishknob is a guru or holy man. He was so interested in talking with you about his cow that he did not notice the old lady and girl. If he had seen them earlier, he would have walked to the other side of the bridge so they could pass without stepping on his shadow."

"What's wrong with them stepping on his shadow?" I interjected.

"Oh, that is very bad." He said.

"For him or for them?"

"For her."

"Why?"

"Because if she had stepped on his shadow, she would have to do many pujas (redemption ceremonies or sacred activities) in order to counteract this sacrilege of lack of respect toward his shadow."

"But" I said, "the Vaishknob would have had no idea that she stepped on his shadow, as he was so engrossed in talking with me."

"He has nothing to do with it. It is her responsibility not to step on his shadow. She is the one who would suffer and have bad karma. She is the one who would have to do the time delaying pujas."

Chapter 14

Like father, like son.

At times, I treated some of the sick animals in some of my study villages. On one occasion, as I was on my way by myself to treat a sick cow during the monsoon season, I was trapped in a down pour of rain of significant proportions. I had taken refuge on the thatched veranda of one of the nearest mud huts. As I sat there by myself, two of the local teenaged boys ran through the rain, jumped up onto the porch, and proceeded to ask me question after question about the United States and capitalism. The government of the state of West Bengal at that time was dominated by elected communists. The boys were very intense and interested. I estimated their ages to be around 14 or 15 years old.

During the question and answer period, each of them used the phrase, ". . . your Jesus would . . ", or ". . . your Jesus says . . . ". After hearing this phrase at least ten times, I said, "By the way, I should tell you that he is not my Jesus because I am not a Christian."

Both of the boys stared at me in utter disbelief and shock. After a very brief period of silence one of the lads became so agitated, that with obvious disgust and hatred in his eyes, he raised his fist and hollered, "You mean that you have forsaken your father's religion?"

I calmly said, "Not everyone in the United States are Christians. The United States citizens constitute a melting pot of the world. There are Jews, Buddhists, Muslims, Hindus, Atheists, and Agnostics; you name it. And, besides that, there are so many other different religions practiced in the U.S."

They became mollified and the questions continued for some time before the rain stopped. The central human informative issue here, is that in India it seems like it is almost a sin to deviate from the philosophical or religious leaning of one's father. It is the same in the United States. I will digress in order to relate a conversation that I had with a fellow student at the University of the South in Sewanee, Tennessee years before.

During my second year at Sewanee (1956 to 1957), a black female, by the name of Autherine Lucy, attempted to integrate the student body of the all-white University of Alabama in Tuscaloosa. She enrolled as a graduate student to pursue a Master's degree in Library Science. On her third day of attending classes, demonstrations and riots broke out against her entering the university.

Immediately, many of the students at Sewanee (then an all-male college) from Alabama were openly talking about leaving school and going down to Tuscaloosa to buy guns and going to defend the status quo of racial segregation. What follows is a brief summary of a conversation that I had with one of these die hard bigoted individuals.

I opened the conversation by asking, "What's so bad about a black person attending college that you feel so strongly that you want to go down there and shoot people?"

He answered, "Black people got no business going to college."

I retorted, "Why do you say that? It seems to me that it is no skin off of your teeth to let blacks get educated."

"They are fine the way they are now. They don't need a college education for what they do."

I pointed out, "What they do is mainly work for white folks. Maybe they would like to get an education and work for themselves and besides, they are just as intelligent as white people with the same education."

"You're wrong Odend'hal. They are not as intelligent as white people," was his answer.

"I think that you are just worried about them working hard and taking some of your prospective jobs. That is the real reason you don't want them to get the same education," I suggested.

He responded, "Okay, I will not argue with you about this. I will not stand for it no matter what you say. I'll tell you the real reason I will not allow no black person to go to college."

"Pray tell, what is the real reason that you do not want, 'no black person to go to college?'"

"Because my daddy and my daddy before him would not allow it." he blurted out.

In disgust I said, "If that is your real reason, that sounds pretty damned stupid to me."

Chapter 15

He's not my brother and she's not my sister.

While I was a graduate student at the University of Missouri – Columbia, I attended a wedding of some friends. At the wedding I saw and struck up a conversation with a lady wearing a sari. She was the wife of one of the Indian physicians in Columbia. I do not remember exactly which Indian state that she was from, but I seem to think that she was from Gujarat. During the conversation, I asked if she knew one of the Indian graduate student by the name of Ram, who was from the Punjab region of India.

Ram was a Hindu Punjabi from the city of Amritsar. I had met him at some of the graduate student parties around town. He was always with another Punjabi female graduate student, Rieta (as I recall), who was a Muslim from the city of Lahore, very near the city of Amritsar. Also, another distinctive difference between these two was the fact that he lived in India and she lived in Pakistan. I knew that this attractive couple had been dating each other for over a year and I often saw them together around the campus.

After I asked the Indian lady in the sari at the wedding if she knew Ram. She answered, "Oh, yes, I know that handsome devil. He is quite bright you know."

"I see Ram with a girl from Lahore a lot." I added.

She beamed with exuberance and conspiratorially, she whispered, "Oh, yes, and did you know (she paused slightly to look around), they might even get married?"

Shocked at her openly ultraliberal attitude, I said, "Gosh, do you know that she is a Muslim from Pakistan and he is a Hindu from India?"

Slightly peeved at my question, she responded, "Of course, I know that (raising her head up a notch). I have known them for some time."

"And doesn't that bother you?" I could not help asking.

"Oh, no. You see, he is not my brother and she is not my sister."

"What if one of them happened to be your brother or your sister?" was my immediate follow up question.

Her expression changed instantly and with her eyes narrowed, she said, "Even the mention of such a thing as marriage would get them severely beaten."

So, as long as the couple was of no direct relationship to her, there would be no shame brought to her family. However, if one of them happened to be a relative, I have read and heard stories of "honor killings" by family members when members of the same family brought shame on the family by trespassing religious dictates and mores of India or Pakistan. This can even occur to rape victims, or for what may first appear to be trivial minor offences from a Westerner's perspectives.

Chapter 16

Mormons think; do you think?

During my graduate school at the University of Missouri-Columbia, I was for a time, in charge of our Sunday service programs for the Unitarian-Universalist Fellowship. Being a fellowship, there was no minister and the entire congregation was lay lead. As is the periodic custom of Unitarian-Universalists, we try to learn as much as possible about other religions and frequently have Jewish rabbis, Christian ministers, Buddhists monks, Hindus gurus and Muslims clerics to come and speak to us at our main Sunday services.

I asked a Mormon veterinary faculty member to come and talk about Mormonism to the congregation. He gave a very interesting and smooth presentation and it was well received. One aspect of Mormon practices that he revealed was the concept of a sacrosanct week day evening; whereby all members of a Mormon family would forgo any outside activities and everybody would always stay at home after dinner. Other admirable customs, such as: the abstinence of the consumption of alcohol, recreational drugs, and smoking cigarettes were also appreciated.

After every presentation, we always allow members of the congregation to ask questions. During the question and answer session, there was a question from the assistant administrator of the University Hospital who happened to be black. He said, "Can you tell me, why is it that the Mormon Church prohibits any black man or woman from serving as a deacon in the Mormon Church?"

My friend and colleague responded, "Well, that is because the Council of Elders who control the policies of the church have decided after divine consultation with God, that it would not be a good idea at this time."

My black Unitarian-Universalist friend then said, "Do you anticipate that in the near future, this policy might be changed?"

My veterinary friend then said, "I'm sorry. I have no control over such a possibility." And the matter came to an end.

After I thanked him for his presentation as he was walking out the front door I shook his hand, but did no let go, even though I sensed that he wanted to make a rapid exit.

I said, "Bob, tell me honestly, what do you think about this exclusion of blacks by the church?"

He looked at me with a hint of surprise and said, "Well, that is not for me to say. It is a matter between the Council of Elders and God."

I quickly interjected, "I am not asking about the Council of Elders or god. I am asking YOU, how do you feel about this policy? Do you think it is fair?"

"As I told you, Stew, I have no say so and cannot question the edicts given by the Council of Elders, as they, not I, have the power to seek guidance from God."

"For Christ's sake, Bob, you are entitled to a personal opinion. I am asking you, do you think the policy is fair?"

"I'm not going to stand here and argue with you about this. I support whatever the Council of Elders decides and I don't want to think about it."

I started to say, 'In other words, you do not want to think period, and you are content to let a bunch of older (possibly senile) men think for you.' But, of course, because of my upbringing, I stifled my impulsive harangue, kept silent, and just thanked him for coming to the Unitarian-Universalist church.

Chapter 17

It depends on what you know.

In 1983, my services were on load to the United States Department of Agriculture (USDA) to participate in a project to fight an outbreak of African swine fever in Haiti. The United States is, and was, free of this dreadful viral disease. While the disease is of no threat to human health directly, it is particularly disastrous to the economy of a disease free country. This is because following the initial infective agent's introduction into a country, due to the length of time before any signs of the disease appeared, the disease would not be diagnosed until months later and would then require drastic and very expensive measures to eradicate it. Therefore, the United States spent 14 million dollars to eradicate the disease in Haiti. If the African swine fever virus had been introduced into the United States by Haitian refugees carrying infected pork, the cost to the United States was calculated to exceed over 14 billion dollars.

Shortly before I left to go to Haiti, an amusing exchange occurred in the faculty lounge at the veterinary school in Georgia. Frank Hayes, a veterinarian who had just returned from Haiti said to me, "Now Stew when you go down to Haiti I want you to be sure and do one thing very religiously for me."

"What's that Frank?"

"When you reach those road blocks leading into the infected areas, I want you to promise me that you will do whatever those little teenaged officers holding the uzi submachine guns tell you to do."

In order to placate his wishes I responded, "Okay Frank, I will do whatever those little teenaged officers holding the uzi submachine guns tell me to do at the road blocks; but only if it is reasonable."

John Williams, another veterinarian laughed heartily and hollered out from the other side of the room, "Hell Odend'hal, if they are holding the uzi submachine guns, everything they say IS reasonable."

The eradication team in Haiti included veterinarians from Mexico, the United States, the Dominican Republic, and Haiti. Two of the veterinarians who worked full time for the USDA were originally from Egypt. I worked in the field with one of them who was a devout Muslim. We traveled all over Haiti and frequently spent the night at agricultural field stations where we each carried out our respective tasks.

At one location, as we entered our assigned room for the night, Mustafa said to me quite casually, "Stew, do you mind if I say my prayers?"

"Of course not Mustafa. Would you prefer me to leave the room?"

"No, that won't be necessary. Please remain. You won't bother or inhibit me at all."

I responded, "Okay. I'll stay then and quietly unpack."

The room was sort of small and had two twin beds which were longitudinally arranged side by side in a North-South direction. As I quietly unpacked, I surreptitiously glanced over to observe Mustafa saying his prayers. I had never been this close to a Muslim when they said their prayers before.

The first thing I noticed was that he placed a towel on the floor between the two twin beds. He stood behind the towel, bowed his head and mumbled a series of very low chants. I could not hear well enough to tell whether or not he spoke in English or Arabic. After a couple of minutes, his next action shocked me.

Whenever I travel, I always make a special effort to be aware of the four basic directions of my surroundings. In this case, even though the sky was slightly over cast and the position of the sun was not discernible, I had been following our general directions on the road map that we were provided. I therefore noticed when we turned off of the main road, that the dormitory where we were staying was oriented in an East – West direction. To my utter amazement, Mustafa kneeled down on the towel with his head pointed due North and not east toward Mecca. Being aware of the extreme sensitivities of the practitioners of Islam, I refrained from any comments or questions and kept the observation to myself.

Weeks later at another location, when Mustafa and I were again alone I nonchalantly asked, "Mustafa, when you say your prayers, do you always have to face Mecca?"

"But, of course." came the immediate reply.

"Well, what happens if you don't face Mecca when you pray?" I timidly continued.

"Oh," he said with strong conviction, "That is very bad."

"What would happen if you accidentally were praying in the wrong direction?"

With a big smile on his face, he looked at me and said in this strong Arabic accent, "If you don't know, it don't matter."

For the rest of my months in Haiti, Mustafa remained his typical jovial, optimistic, kind and thoughtful characteristic self. I thought to myself, Mustafa must have been correct in his assessment of no punishment from Allah for his unknowing transgression since no adverse catastrophes were inflicted upon him.

Chapter 18

Whose belief are you going to believe?

While teaching at the veterinary school in Georgia, an international graduate student, who was from the Luo tribe in Kenya, came into my office. He was literally crying tears because he said, "I come here to learn how to help my country. And all I learn about is about puppy dogs and kitty cats. When I go back to my country, they will think I am mad."

I explained to him that the situation was temporary and he would soon learn about the diseases and parasites of large animals as well later on. The poor guy was so disturbed, that it took some time to calm him down.

I finally said, "Look, why don't you come to my house for dinner this evening? Just come back to my office at 5:30 and I will give you a ride to my house and then take you back to your dorm afterward."

He immediately agreed.

At lunch time that same day, I strolled downtown and stopped at a magazine shop and bought the latest issue of the Natural History magazine because it displayed a Masai warrior (also from Kenya) on the cover holding a spear. Back at my office, I devoured the article in 15 minutes.

In the article, it stated that the members of the Masai tribe do not believe that they are stealing cattle from the surrounding tribes when they raid the other tribes to take their cattle. This is because they believe that god gave them all of the cattle in the world, and they are just taking back what rightfully belongs to them.

That evening at my house after dinner I showed this article to the Luo graduate student and let him read the high-lighted passage about the Masai believing that god gave them all of the cattle of the world.

He read it and then said loudly, "Oh, ho, ho, Luo believe the same thing!"

Perplexed, thinking that he approved of the Masai's belief statement, I blurted out, "Huh?"

"Oh yeah, the Luo believe the same thing. That is, the Luo believe that when we attack another tribe to confiscate their cattle, we are just taking back what rightfully belongs to us, because we believe that god gave us all of the cattle of the world."

I said, "Since the two beliefs are diametrically opposed to one another, one must obviously conclude that somebody's god is wrong."

Chapter 19

A little twig will do ya.

As president of the University of Georgia chapter of the Society for International Development, I asked a Unitarian-Universalist couple that I knew to give a talk on their experiences as Peace Corps volunteers in the West African country of Ghana.

During the talk, they showed a slide of a very small plot of cultivated land surrounded by forest. At one side of the plot, there were two small twigs bound together in the form of a cross stuck in the ground.

The wife of the team said, "See that twig at the edge of the field? That is their security system. It prevents anyone from stealing any food from that plot."

A roar of laughter filled the lecture room. Everybody just knew that the twig could not hold back anyone intent on stealing the crop.

"No, no", she protested vigorously, "you just do not understand. It works. This is because of their beliefs. If anyone steals the food with the twig being there, they believe an evil curse will ruin their life. And the belief is so strong, that no one messes with the crop."

"What about, if someone pulls the twig out in the middle of the night and then steals the food?" someone interjected.

"That won't happen either for the same reason. So what you all laugh at, with your back ground, has no relevance to what they believe in their culture. What works in one culture has no effect in another."

Chapter 20
You have to hand it to some religions.

In April of 1985 I presented a paper at a conference on viral diseases in Rabat, the capitol city of Morocco. The brother of a graduate student at the University of Georgia was driving me around the city to show me the local areas of interest. Wherever he parked his car, he always gave some small coins to a man in the area to look after his car (presumably to keep it safe). On three separate consecutive occasions, the man that was supposed to look after his car had no right hand. Following the third time this happened, I said to the brother of my friend back in Athens, "Don't you think that it is ironic that you are giving money to a thief to watch after your car?"

Showing obvious surprise, "What do you mean?" was his response.

"Well, I noticed that each of the people that you gave the money to, had no right hand. So they must have been a thief, right?"

"No, no. They lost their hand in the war." he protested.

I persisted, "What war?"

"Oh, you know; the war."

"No, I don't know. What war?"

"The war. The war. It was the war." he continued with demonstrable irritation. I decided to drop any further questioning. But I doubt very seriously that they lost their hand in "the war". I strongly suspect that those people were suspected of being a thief and as sharia law (the Islamic code of law that is based on the Koran) dictates, their right hand was chopped off.

Chapter 21

What is the difference between science and religion?

Science seeks the truth by trial and error empirically. Science does not try to undermine the credibility of religion. Religion does it all by itself, by preposterous claims. Homo sapiens do not need freedom **of** religion. Homo sapiens need freedom **from** religion.

Religions leaders and adherents usually study the past and argues about it and try to determine "religious truths" (an oxymoron) that support unknowable or ridiculous positions. Science studies the present and tries to make accurate predictions about the future and cooperates with others to determine truisms. Many religions are adversarial and confrontational. Each separate group makes unsubstantiated claims of the "truth" and attacks those who disagree. Science is based on the mutual discovery of "truth" by trial and error which can eventually seek rules and laws about existence and reality.

Several religions generate emotional anger and hatred toward others. Science seeks to find justification of competing theories by thinking and collegiality. Often religious leaders dictate fuzzy logic to the masses by impossible to prove creeds and threatens retribution to anyone who questions their authority. Science sometimes have proponents who advocate erroneous theories, but with open discussion and thinking in the aggregate, the erroneous theories are corrected and natural laws are eventually discovered.

Most religions seem to stifle all dissent. Science, on the other hand welcomes dissent as a necessary part of progress toward revealing basic laws of reality. Religions attack and attempt to diminish scientific facts. Science merely points out inconsistencies of religious claims that contradict basic natural laws of existence.

Religions do not seem to like questions, while science loves questions. How does one learn, if questions are not allowed? Religion does not want the masses to think. Science, asks the masses to think.

It is easy to demonstrate the stupidity of radical fundamentalists doctrine, but difficult to criticize scientific laws. Contrast the Christian claim that Jesus was born of the Virgin Mary, with the eventual scientific discovery that it is the earth's spin that accounts for the fact that the sun comes up in the east every morning. Shall we just say that there are some obvious misgivings about the veracity of the Christian's claim of the Virgin Mary compared to the scientific explanation of why the sun comes up every morning in the east. Which is more credible?

Compare the results of religious activity and accomplishments with those of science. Religion provides psychological comfort to the adherents, but also stimulates division, distrust and hatred toward those who are different. Science also provides psychological comfort to adherents by means of discovery, not dictatorial edicts from the clergy. Instead of distrust and hatred of those who differ from each other, there is a fervent desire to rectify the conflicting ideas and reach a compromise or seek the truth by empirical scientific investigation and testing; not philosophical arguments impossible to substantiate.

Religion is analog (fuzzy and unclear); science is digital (sharp, clear and precise). Religion is divisive; science is cooperative. Religion looks to and studies the past; science proves the present and more accurately predicts the future. Religion asks the masses to obey and not ask questions and above all, asks them not to think; science asks the masses to ask questions and to think for themselves.

With which group would you rather be associated: a group that demands unthinking blind obedience and disseminated radical hatred toward others; or a group that strives to discover reproducible tested truths that have had immediate positive benefits to the population at large? Which group would you trust the most?

Chapter 22

What happens to Muslim women when they die?

I was in a book store in Albuquerque, New Mexico when I saw a Muslim woman wearing a head scarf with a very young child. I walked up to the woman and said, "Do you mind if I ask you a question?"

She replied, "No. Go ahead."

"I was just wondering about something. I have read parts of the Koran translated into English and it says that when men die they are rewarded in heaven with 72 virgins. What does the Koran say about women when they die? Certainly, they are not rewarded with 72 virgins."

"Oh, gosh. I just do not know." Then after a slight pause she continued, "I think that when I die, if I love my husband; I will be with him." Another slight pause occurred and she said (perhaps wishful thinking), "However, if I do not love my husband, I probably will not have to be with him."

Before I could say anything her husband walked up and said to me in a very pleasant manner, "Can I help you?"

I responded with, "I was just asking your wife if she knew what happened to Muslim women when they died according to the Koran, because I read in the Koran that men were rewarded with 72 virgins in heaven when they died. Do you know what the Koran says about what happens to women when they die?"

He sort of scratched his head and said, "You know, I have no idea. The thought never occurred to me before."

I guess what amazed me more than anything was the fact that he did not know and apparently did not care what the Koran had to say about women who died.

If one asks the same question on any internet search browser, there are a number of conflicting answers.

Chapter 23

Discussion and Summary

Upon reflection of my early childhood, undoubtedly I was affected by religion as I was growing up. To begin with it was a positive influence and I considered the ministry as a possible career. As I matured, I became disenchanted with the obvious falsehoods of the dogmatic creeds and rituals. During my education, it became clear to me that humans are really just another animal endowed with certain advantages and disadvantages similar to all specific species.

Do animals have religion? Do animals have abstract thinking? Does it really matter whether they do or do not? I do not think that animals worry about gods, demons, angels, heaven, hell and sin. That some humans worry about those things results in a calamity for our species because of the induction of the concept of "them and us". This fosters elitism and distrust of those who do not agree with a particular brand of religion. It is the source of wars and hated. Religion is divisive and not cooperative. It inculcates fear and anxiety.

I now consider myself an inquisitive dubious atheistic agnostic. The path to that particular loose label has involved several rocky roads and unique experiences.

When I was a child, I had the experience to attend several different protestant churches which were all similar flavors of the same Christian package. Luckily, my grandmother exposed me to the more logical and truthful message of the Unitarian church.

As a senior in high school I did not want to take the more difficult course of physics and opted for a course in "Christian ethics". During that course my friend, Jay Bernstein, and I went to a different church every Sunday during the semester and reported on our impressions to the instructor.

One of the amazing things to me was that on one occasion we went to the largest Baptist Church in Oklahoma City. It occupied a square city block consisting of a cathedral and a sports complex. Across the street there was a book store in a building that was at least 8 stories high which also belonged to the church. The day that we happened to attend the Sunday service, all they talked about was their need for more money to expand their church.

Parenthetically, I want to express my distaste on the injudicious practice by governments of not charging any property taxes on the land owned by churches. Furthermore, the Internal Revenue Service should not allow tax deductions for religious contributions. If these monetary resources could be directed more to the common good than to the special interest groups, it would decrease our national debt and could be used for more worthwhile purposes.

I have experienced many miraculous-like events in my life, such as the birth of my children, the ecstasy of sex and love; the awe inspiring beauty of natural landscapes, etc. All of these wonderful experiences can be explained by natural occurrences. None of them require divine interventions. Even those miraculous-like events of my youth can later on be easily explained by natural phenomena.

During my journey to religious disillusionment, I learned about the plasticity and power of the brain. Atheists, theists and agnostics, all can rationalize any and everything if they so choose. Prayers, intense concentrations, meditations, and many others supplications techniques can result in the complete certainty that a higher power has responded to your desires. However, just as with the effects of placebos, alcohol and drugs, a logical explanation can be found. Prayers are sometime answered by imagination and self-generated will power.

With regard to the Apostles' Creed, I personally believe nothing stated in the creed, but the death of Christ. The rest is impossible to believe. Alleged by some that it was the writings of the individual 12 apostles; this has been discounted early in its distribution. Apparently, it originated in a letter from a council in Milan, Italy to the Pope in the year 390 A.D. (or C.E., meaning the Current Era). Following many revisions, Charlemagne popularized it during his reign in France.

The Nicene Creed was an area of disagreement in which there was an attempted to come to a compromise to establish the basic beliefs of various Christian factions. In the city of Nicaea in Turkey in the year of 325

C. E., the first ecumenical council developed it. Like the Apostles' Creed, its statements defy natural laws and is impossible to rectify with reality. As a young child reciting these creeds surrounded by adults, the deeper meaning of the words were not an issue. At that age, one is forced to think that the adults know best and therefore, one emulates those mature individuals whom one believes to be more erudite. When maturity sets in and greater personal responsibility becomes necessary, one develops a more critical assessments of one's beliefs and actions.

The statement that only a fool does not change his mind, is instructive. After thinking about the Apostles' Creed and the Nicene Creed, I would be a fool if I did not recognize that the messages are devoid of reality and without any foundation. Years later, after a few of my friends knew that I regularly attended the Unitarian church, they would ask me about our beliefs. I would tell them that we have no creed. That we belief in the inherent value of every living thing and that we study all of the religions of the world seeking the best practices taught by those different religions. We are not evangelistic, but accept anyone interested in furthering their understanding of some of the mysteries of life. As a result, I personally have had devout Christians come to me and ask if they could attend the Unitarian church because they also had legitimate doubts as to the tenets of the Christian church's basic beliefs.

I love the statement that, "You can make no generalizations; including this one." Obviously, you can attempt to characterize some entities by general statements, but they always need to be qualified and defined rigidly. However, it seems to me that fundamentalists of all religions are fundamentally ignorant of the basic laws of nature. Otherwise, they would not be fundamentalists and have the views they have. To repeat again, the American humorist (Will Rogers) from Oklahoma once said that, "Everyone is ignorant; just on different subjects." It amazes me that many religions do not want to learn anything outside of the history of their own religion. They remain ignorant of other religions and just look for things to criticize.

There is no sense in arguing with fundamentalists. They only have a transmitter, but no receiver. As Thomas Paine said, "To argue with someone who has renounced reason, is like giving medicine to a dead person."

Many religions inculcate fear by assigning sin to natural biological urges. With the introduction of this fear, the clerics try to control and intimidate their flock. Further, they try and invent fantastic farfetched fabricated falsehoods like heaven and hell to "put the fear of God" into their adherent's psyche.

Growing older and becoming increasingly disenchanted with most religions, the propaganda of the media to promote and perpetuate religious lore irritated me. Whether it is radio, movies, newspapers, magazines or other multimedia devises, the messages seemed to support unrealistic ideas from the Bible. The general population seemed to equate the word "atheist" with the devil and anyone who might have suggested that atheism was not evil, was unpatriotic to the American ideal. While I eventually considered myself as an agnostic, I felt that this characterization of atheists is unfair and presents a much distorted picture. Even to this day, I recently read where there is only one single admitted atheist in the United States congress. It is disconcerting to me to know that people who control our government are mainly religious adherents who avoid logical thinking and are dedicated to religious distortions of the truth.

The evolution of religions have followed a certain tract. Primitive tribes worshiped the sun because they knew how important and necessary it was for their survival. The Greeks had many gods (Zeus, the supreme god; Ares, the god of war; Aphrodite, the god of love, etc.). Hindus, as well, have many gods to this day.

The more recent three major monotheistic religions of Jews, Christians and Muslims claim to be the ultimate true religions and the most recent evolutionary manifestation of divinity. It is ironic that these three religions are the most aggressive and warlike not only toward each other, but toward all other religions. One only has to acknowledge: the Irish catholic vs protestants; then in India, the Hindus vs Muslims; in the Middle East, the Sunnis vs the Shia and of course, there was the crusades in the middle ages, as well as the inquisition.

Religions cultivate lies, as the little Muslim boy undoubtedly learned to lie after the episode described in Chapter 11. Christ was not the only holy man who was claimed to have been conceived by a god spirit.

Parthenogenesis is possible in insects and other arthropods, but clearly impossible in primates. Jesus was not born in December. He was allegedly born in March because of the astronomical profile of the sky at that time. Years after his death, the leaders of the Christian church decided to take a pagan celebration of the Winter solstice (festival of lights) and redirect and rename it as the celebration of Christmas (just another lie). This festival of lights is prominent in many other religions, i.e. Jewish Hanukkah and Hindu Diwali.

What you see can hurt you (Chapter 13) and a little twig will do ya (Chapter 19), illustrate what anthropologists and psychologists have known for centuries. Life viewed through the colored and distorted lens of one cultural perspective can be deceiving and offensive in another cultural setting. Religions constitute nothing more than ethnic and/or tribal norms. Individuals embedded within the constraints of specific groups can no longer remain in them if they break the accepted taboos and behavior patterns of the majority. If they do, they become outcasts, are shunned or attacked as deviants. Several examples reveal how subtle infractions can result in misunderstanding and animosity.

When I lived in Australia, occasionally while visiting people's houses, I had asked to use their telephone to make a quick phone call to other friends. The householder would usually immediately grant me permission to do so. After living there for almost a year, I heard (by the grape vine, i.e. snippets of comments and/or rumors) that so-in-so considered me to be a particularly rude and thought-less individual.

I considered this characterization to be unwarranted and without any foundation because I thought that I usually went out of my way to be sensitive to everybody around me. After some time of hearing these accusations, one person was kind enough to explain that the major complaint had to do with the fact that I used other people's telephone in their homes and never bothered to pay for using the telephone.

What I did not know was, that in Australia (unlike in the United States) homeowners were charged money for each and every individual local telephone call. I had just assumed that everybody paid a set monthly price for the use of the phone and one could make as many local telephone calls as they wanted and there was no charge for individual telephone calls.

Since I did not offer to pay for using the householder's phone for the telephone call, I was deemed rude. Once this was explained to me, I went out of my way to apologize to those whom I had offended and explained my cultural background, relative to telephone use in America.

In Calcutta (now called Kolkata) India, I met a couple from the University of Chicago who were both completely fluent in the Bengali language. They were both very aware of most of the dos and don'ts of Bengali etiquette and dressed as native Bengalis did. Whereas, I, who was immediately recognized by my western attire as a foreigner, would be forgiven for minor breaches of etiquette, they, at times, were severely admonished for their slip of adherence to these same minor transgressions. The Bengalis knew that I didn't know any better, but were shocked to see the Chicago couple make the same mistake, because they were so prefect in their Bengali dress and manners that the Bengalis thought that they should have known better.

Shortly, after returning from India having lived there for over a two year period, I had a strange experience at an Indian restaurant in Washington, D.C... When I first went to India many people (both Indians and Americans) told me to sit on my left hand whenever I go out to dinner. This was because most Indians when they go to the toilet use their left hand and water to clean their anus after defecating. They do not use toilet paper. Therefore, most Indians refrain from using their left hand when eating or drinking. If they see someone else eat with their left hand, it is disgusting to them. I subconsciously must have adopted this same mindset. At the Washington D.C. Indian restaurant I observed an American pick up a piece of chicken with their left hand and was immediately repulsed. At the time, I remember thinking that it was so interesting that such alien cultural habits can be learned and embedded by repetition.

While we are on the subject of cross cultural misunderstandings, I should mention three other brief examples. In the men's restroom in the American Consulate in Calcutta, if you happened to go into one of the toilet stalls and shut the door, you would see the following sign prominently displayed on the back of the door: "EMPLOYEES FOUND WITH THEIR FEET ON THE TOILET SEAT WILL BE FIRED". This was because most Indians were used to their toilets which consisted usually of two foot prints on either side of a hole. Therefore, the Indian employees thought that putting their bottom where someone else's bottom had been placed before them was very unhygienic.

Speaking of cultural hygienic differences, the cleaning of the nasal passages was another area of mutual disgust. Bengalis would say that to blow your nose into a clean cloth and then stick the icky sticky mucus coated snot with boogers back into your pocket and walk around all day with that junk in your pocket was disgusting. By the same token, their habit was abhorrent to westerners. The Bengali practice (at that time) was to place one finger over one nostril, take a deep breath, and then blow the contents of the other nasal passage out so strongly that they could accurately direct the contents to the side of a wall, or on to a chosen spot on the pavement of a sidewalk or the floor of a building. I frequently would see these "honkers" displayed on the walls and floors of the All India Institute of Hygiene and Public Health (in those days) in Calcutta.

Parenthetically, I must add that in the 1960s during the Viet Nam war, the elected communist government in Calcutta renamed the street that the American Consulate was on. They changed the name from Harrington Street to Ho Chi Minh Sarani.

In most cultures of the world, it is considered a great transgression to go against the religious or familial attitudes (particularly the father), as presented in Chapters 14 and 15. This fact is interesting from the point of view of what I observed in China. China is not a religious country. One of the main roles of societal stability is ancestor worship. Also, Confucianism is not a religion. It involves rules for social harmony, where each individual person concentrates on self-improvement, by striving to emulate the "superior man". That is, Confucianism urges all citizens to live by rules that allow for good works and good government.

The following anecdote illustrates the long lasting influence and the power of ancestor worship. The village that I studied in China was called Fengjiacun in the province of Shandong. There was no cemetery in or near the village. When inhabitants died, they were cremated and some of their remains were buried near the intersection of the main road of the village connecting to the road leading to a larger county town. Next to the ditches that bordered the road there were these cones of earth which varied from

2 inches to 2 feet tall. Some of these cones had a small rock placed on top and others did not. The cones just looked like powdered earth that had been formed from dirt that was allowed to be carefully and gently dropped from above. When I asked about why the cremated remains were buried there, I was told that there was no room for a cemetery because of the limited land which was needed for growing food.

However, once I noticed an easel like structure holding a large wreath in the middle of a very large recently plowed field with flowers surrounding the base of it. When I asked about it, I was told that it was the ancestral land of someone whose ashes were recently buried there. I said that I was told the ashes of people who died in Fengjiacun were buried near the main road. They said that yes that was true, except some of the ashes were saved and following the ceremony for the burial at the intersection, there had to be another ceremony to bury some of the remains on their ancestral land.

I was surprised at this last explanation because all of the land was owned by the state government since the communist revolution back in the late 1940s. So, I said, "Gosh, it has been over 40 years since there was any ancestral land, since the government owns all of the land. I mean this memorial is in the middle of this vast field, so how do the family members know where their ancestral land is with no demarcations in sight?"

The immediate answer was, "Everybody knows where their ancestral land is."

As another villager there in Fengjiacun told me once, "Old habits die hard."

Chapter 16 illustrates how devotees are reluctant to think and avoid challenging the precepts of their religion. Some clergy want to be in charge and control the flock for their own benefit. If you want to see how living under a theocratic state is so distorted read the following books about the present state of Iran (Elliot 2006, Saberi 2010, Serov 2008).

Most religions have gurus, ministers, preachers, imams, prophets, emissaries, etc., to study and reveal their "religious truths". Most religious people wish to abide by the dictates of their creeds. It is easy and they do not have to think. Therefore, the path of least resistance is to go along with the crowd, no matter where the crowd is going or not thinking. Thus, the adherents are mired in the past and prisoners of their respective erroneous mind sets.

The Baha'i religion has the latest prophet, Baha'u'llah. He arose in Iran in the mid – 1800s. To his credit, he stipulated that there should be no clergy. However, devotees have to mention his name at least 95 times a day. But this is still an improvement over the earlier religions which gave such corrosive powers to members of the elite bishops, ministers and other higher-ups.

Chapter 17 demonstrates that there are many behaviors that are not tolerated by many religions. So, not only do you not have to think, you can fail to honor and keep the dictated behavior patterns and go against them anyway, as long as you are ignorant of your own transgressions. What a nice escape valve. Then, of course, even if you know you are breaking the laws of the church, all you have to do is go see a priest, confess your sins and gain redemption by following the advice of the priest to whom you confessed.

Chapter 18 is a perfect example of illustrating how each religion's leaders use the name of god as an excuse to justify anything, no matter how irrational it may be. Muhammad allegedly took extra wives using the excuse that god told him it was all right. This was done with no witnesses or notary public verification. Cult leaders do the same thing in modern times. The demonization of other tribes and religions allows for the justification of killing other groups. Sordid behaviors by holy men are hidden by the power structures of the Catholic Church and others. The list of offences and criminal activity perpetrated by the clergy are habitually shielded from public view. A book, I do recommend everyone to read is *"In God's Name"* (Yallop 2007). However, be forewarned that it will destroy the reader's faith in the Vatican, as it was written by a former Vatican priest.

Catholic sex crimes are due entirely to the unnatural ludicrous idea of having the priests "celebrate" celibacy. Sex is a natural appetite, just like for food, otherwise we all would not be here. To have normal sex prohibited, causes the problem of "father's" (an oxymoron), i.e. Catholic priests, abusing little boys and girls, which is despicable. Compounding the problem is the fact that the, so called, (allegedly) holy men in charge of this religion have tried to sweep the truth under the rug. If these leaders were educated to the imperatives of the field of biology and priests were allowed to marry a great deal of the problem would most likely disappear.

Chapter 19 provides two lessons. One is: that if everybody believes something so intensely, it is honored and works no matter how ridiculous it might appear to outsiders. Two is: memes can be dangerous or wonderful following their indoctrination. Memes are the viral-like inculcated thoughts introduced to a human that infect one person, who then infects those around him or her, which eventually cause a chain reaction of infecting the entire group (Dawkins 1989).

I personally saw foot bound older women in my study village of Fengjiacun in China between 1987 and 1990. What a horrible example of a custom or a meme that started apparently from the common people attempting to emulate a foot fetish prevalent in the "so called" nobility. A reason given to me by one of the local villagers was that foot binding allowed the men to control the women more easily because they could not run away. What amazed me the most was the fact that the process created excruciating pain throughout the whole process and women who had gone through it decided to subject their own daughters to the same agonal procedure. The human brain is a remarkable organ that sometimes can be unbelievably unpredictable.

Chapter 20 demonstrates that the three most notable monotheistic religions are the most violent. Jewish laws stipulated the stoning of adulteresses. Christians had their little inquisition fling and Muslims chop off the hands of suspected thieves. A short review of the essentials of Shari law is instructive because it is now being introduced into American court cases which deal with any of the 8 million Muslims said to live in the United States today (2015).

Shari law is more of an all-encompassing code of conduct of behavior for Muslims. It is based upon the Koran (Quran) and the Sunna. The Koran is the holy book that is the word of the prophet Muhammad and the Sunna is using Muhammad's life style as an example for all Muslims to emulate. The knowledge of Muhammad's life style is based upon the Hadith. The Hadith has to do with the written reports of oral statements made about Muhammad's teachings, deeds, and sayings. The trouble is, many of these reports were first written down many years after the statements had passed through many different individuals. Anyone skilled in local gossip knows how such means of "truthful" communication can become skewed.

It is also of interest to realize that Islam has many denominations similar to the fractionation of Christianity. There are Sunnis, Shia, Wahhabis, and Ibadis for example. Each of these have different interpretations of the Hadith. The personal observation of those poor retches in Morocco, with no right hand, literally turned my stomach.

What are the major differences between humans and other animals? Actually, not a great deal, since there are other animals that have a language (Whales and porpoises) and are tool users (chimpanzees and crows). It is claimed that humans possess greater thinking power which makes us smarter than "lower" animals. Well, I happen to have a bird feeder outside of our breakfast room window. It is amazing how smart the squirrels are to successfully invade and steal the bird feed, no matter how hard I try to prevent them from doing so. Therefore, it would be appropriate to say that the squirrels are smarter than I am. Actually, that does not hurt my feelings at all.

Abstract thinking is another area where humans are said to have a monopoly in the animal kingdom. How on earth do the claimants know what animals are thinking? Then there is the concept of God, or gods, depending upon your individual attachment to one of an estimated 34,000 different religions currently on earth. As I was growing up, my god at the time, declared that humans were **_HIS_** special interest and they were more important to **_HIM_** than anything else in the world. What arrogance!

In high school, when I was the manager of our football team, during the pep talks before the big games, the coach would always say a prayer, asking for god to help us become victorious over the opposing team. I thought to myself at the time, 'Gosh, I feel sorry for god, because the coach of the other team is probably saying the same prayer to his god (often, most likely the same god). And, if it was the same god, it must be tough on him, her, or it, to make a decision on which team to help out the most (unless he had a proxy betting for him on one team in Las Vegas).

Before I summarize my evolutionary journey toward disillusionment with most religions, I want to say, "There, but for the grace of god, go I."

Perhaps, if I had remained at the University of the South and graduated from there, I would not have written this book, because at the University of the South, I was required to attend chapel every day and go to a certain number of Sunday church services per semester. More than likely, upon graduation, I would have joined an Episcopal church in the community where I lived and worked and would have been surrounded by like-minded people whom I enjoyed and socialized with on a regular basis. I doubt very seriously whether or not I would have chosen to challenge the church's teachings and incur the disfavor of friends from my support group. Even if I had some discomfort and misgivings about some of the dogmas, the safest position would be to just keep these opinions to myself. Therefore, we may all become prisoners of our respective cultures (religions) and sub-cultures.

The vast majority of religious people around the world are basically well intentioned decent people. The main problem originates with the "holier than thou" rigid fundamentalists who are intolerant of those who do not follow their distorted view of reality.

I am a firm believer in the idea that a normal bell shaped curve is representative of any animate or inanimate population. It does not matter whether or not one is discussing professions, actors, rocks, geographical topographies, painters, singers, etc.; about 5 to 10 % of the individual units will be excellent and the same percentages will apply to the worst at the other end of the curve. Between these two extremes, the majority of individuals will constitute the average. The curve can easily be skewed one way or the other at times.

The major problem in religion is the extreme fundamentalists who are intolerant of anyone who challenges their beliefs and spread death threats to anyone who is different. These fundamentalists become the terrorists who infect memes of hatred to their true believers toward any non-believer.

It seems to me that there is a desperate need to develop programs to instill a more rational approach to creeds and oaths of the followers of all religions. Exaggerated claims of miracles and other divine interventions should be revised, so that even a fifth grade average student could be aware that the claims or oaths do not exceed the physical laws of nature.

Therefore, a critical means of improving the awareness of the general public depends upon the educational system. I have read in newspapers and magazines where Christians have hidden their religious identities in order to infiltrate the local education board, so that they can have a voice to attack the teaching of evolution. This may be one reason why many Christian denominations have their own schools and colleges throughout the United States.

When I taught students at Johns Hopkins University, the University of Missouri and the University of Georgia, I always stressed that the students should not memorize facts, but should connect the facts to other aspect of a thought or condition so that the facts made sense. This way they could understand and retain the significance of the thought or condition much better. So, a fact based honest education is the key to reduce fairy tale stories that defy logic and serve to improve the lives of future average citizens.

Now to recapitulate my life time journey. When I was a child I believed that the adults around me were much more intelligent than me. Therefore, I followed their lead and believed whatever they told me. As I approached my teenage years, I became somewhat disenchanted about the veracity of some of the stories. At the Unitarian Church, the allegorical nature of the stories mollified my doubts to a degree. At the university level, it was clear that many of the stories were impossible to believe. After formal education, my previous experiences which I may have deemed examples of divine intervention, could be logically explained by natural phenomena. As I entered retirement, I scrutinized the pros and cons of many religions and determined that the world might probably be better off without them than with them.

So, which religions are the exception and not a disillusionment to me? Buddhism, Unitarian-Universalism and Baha'ism; each for different reasons. Buddhism has no god, Unitarian-Universalist can take one or leave one, as you like; and Bahai's have a god, but no clergy. As far as I know, none of these religions have ever started hate campaigns, inquisitions, witch hunts, or wars. Each of them have a mission to improve the now of all people of the earth regardless of their religious beliefs. The Unitarian-Universalists have, instead of a creed, 7 basic principles:

1. The inherent worth and dignity of every person.
2. Justice, equity and compassion in human relations.
3. Acceptance of one another and encouragement of spiritual growth.
4. A free and responsible search for truth and meaning.
5. The right of conscience and use of the democratic process.
6. The goal of world community with peace, liberty, and justice for all.
7. Respect for the independent web of all existence of which we are a part (Cherry 2017).

Conclusions

I had originally entitled this book, *I am a Happy, Contented, Constantly Inquisitive, Slightly Atheistic Agnostic*. Let us take this original title of this book and work backwards. AGNOSTIC (one who believes that there is no proof of the existence of God, but does not deny the possibility that God may exist). If I do not know about the existence of God, what do I know? I know that the sum total of my previous existence in this one life time that I know of, there is more convincing evidence that God does not exist compared to the opposite possibility. Hence, based upon logic and scientific irrefutable determinations, I am SLIGHTLY ATHEISTIC. If I had to wager a bet in Las Vegas or Monti Carlo, I would bet dollars to doughnuts that God does not exit.

I also know that due to the accident of my birth that my parents provided me with a satisfactory supply of intact and appropriate genes. My original geographical setting allowed me to enjoy a robust setting of a loving family and community which encouraged me to work toward higher educational experiences because of my CONSISTANTLY INQUISITIVE nature.

I am HAPPY and CONTENTED because early on, I adopted a statement that has served me well throughout my life. I modified it to be consistent with my characteristic liberal egalitarian beliefs. That statement is: May fate grant me the power to change those things that I can change; the serenity to accept those things that I cannot change; and the wisdom to distinguish between the two. That has been my mantra everywhere I have been in this world.

I doubt very seriously that there is a spiritual world waiting to greet me upon my death. This does not bother me at all. This fact just motivates me to enjoy every moment that I am still breathing. I strive to make those around me happy to be with me and I derive pleasure by making them laugh and enjoy life. Believe it or not, I do not fear death. It is an inevitable part of all living entities. I happen to be an incurable optimist.

WHY do I promote AGNOSTICISM? Because I firmly believe that it is a more honest and truthful appreciation of the human condition, than the indecisive speculation of either deism or atheism, both of which ultimately are characterized as exercises of futility. Further, why did I take the time to undertake the process of writing this book and then go through all of the usual potential rejections from legitimate book publishers? I don't need the money and I don't care about the recognition since I shall soon enough be dead anyway. I did it because in some small way I genuinely would like to make an attempt at making this a better world.

NOW DEAR READER WHAT DO YOU THINK ABOUT BIRTH, LIFE, DEATH AND GOD AFTER HONEST REFLECT UPON THE CONTENTS OF THIS BOOK?

References

Andrews, Seth 2013. *Deconverted: A Journey from Religion to Reason.* Outskirts Press. Parker, Colorado ***

Barber, Nigel 2012. *Why Atheism Will Replace Religion: The Triumph of Earthly Pleasures Over Pie in the Sky.* Nigel Barber, Birmingham, AL ***

Budziszewski, J. 2003. *What We Can't Not Know.* Ignatius Press, San Francisco. 269 pp

Carter, Joseph H. 1991. *Never Met a Man I Didn't Like: The Life and Writings of Will Rogers.* Avon Books, NY *** ***

Cherry, Eric 2017. *The Edict of Torda, a Landmark in Religious Freedom.* UU World 31 (4):45-46.

Dalton, Brian Keith 2015. *Atheist Fundamentalist.* Brian Dalton 19pp

Dawkins, Richard 1989. T*he Selfish Gene*, Oxford University Press, NY. 360 pp

Dawkins, Richard 2006. *The God Delusion*, Bantam Books NY ***

du Sautoy, Marcus 2016. *What We Cannot Know: From Consciousness to the Cosmos, the Cutting Edge of Science Explained.* Harper Collins. London 440 pp

Elliot, Jason 2006. *Mirrors of the Unseen: Journeys in Iran.* Picador, NY ***

Huxley, Julian 1956. *Religion without Revelation.* The New American Library, NY. 222 pp

Kahneman, Daniel 2011. *Thinking Fast and Slow;* Farrar, Straus and Giroux, NY. 500 pp

Kneale, Matthew 2014. *An Atheist's History of Belief.* Counter Point. Berkeley, CA. 251 pp

Navabi, Armin 2014. *Why There is No God.* Atheist Republic 127 pp

Odend'hal, Stewart 1972. *Energetics of Indian Cattle in Their Environment.* Human Ecology 1: 3 – 22.

Odend'hal, Stewart 1979A. *Testing Rodents with Virus Infection Associated (VIA) Antigen Following a Foot and Mouth Disease Epizootic.* Veterinary Record, 104:262

Odend'hal, Stewart 1979B. *On the Sacred Cow Controversy.* Current Anthropology 26:485

Odend'hal, Stewart 1980A. *Human and cattle Population Changes in Deltaic West Bengal India Between 1967 and 1977.* Human Ecology 8:1-7

Odend'hal, Stewart 1980B. *Cattle Ecology of Upland and deltaic Areas of West Bengal.* Tropical Animal Health and Production 12:1-10

Odend'hal, Stewart 1981A. *Comments on Sacred Cows and Water Buffalo in India.* Current Anthropology 22:497

Odend'hal, Stewart 1981B, *Unusual Rat Feeding Behavior Associated with Cattle Affected with Foot and Mouth Disease.* The Journal of the Bombay Natural History Society 77:317-318

Odend'hal, Stewart 1982A. *Comments on Bovine Sex and Species Ratios in India.* Current Anthropology 23:378

Odend'hal, Stewart 1982B. *Bovine Leukosis in Native and Crossbred Cattle in West Bengal.* Indian Veterinary Journal 59:72-73

Odend'hal, Stewart 1986. *Bovine Leukosis: An Example of Poor Disease Monitoring in International Livestock Shipments to Developing Countries.* Social Science and Medicine 23:1017-1020

Odend'hal, Stewart 1988A. *Human and Cattle Population Changes in Deltaic West Bengal, India between 1977 and 1987.* Human Ecology 16:23-33

Odend'hal, Stewart 1988B. *Human and Cattle Population Changes in Upland West Bengal, India, between 1977-78 and 1987.* Human Ecology 16:145-155

Odend'hal, Stewart and Brown, John 1988. *Relative Energetic Efficiencies of Milk Production in Village India by Crossbred and Native Cattle.* National Geographic Research 4:540-547

Rizvi, Ai A. 2016. *The Atheist Muslim: A Journey from Religion to Reason.* St. Martin's Press, NY ***

Russell, Bertram 1957. *Why I am Not a Christian.* Simon & Schuster, NY

Saberi, Roxana 2010. *Between two worlds: My Life and Captivity in Iran.* HaperCollins e-books, NY ***

Serov, Banafsheh 2008. *Under a Starless Sky: A Family's Escape from Iran.* Hachette. Sydney, Australia ***

Tolle, Eckhart 2006. *A New Earth: Awakening to Your Life's Purpose.* First Plume Printing. London. 316 pp

Warraq, Ibn 2003. *Leaving Islam: Apostates Speak Out.* Prometheus Books, Amherst, NY ***

Williams, Albert 2014. *Why Our Children Will Be Atheists*: The Last 100 years of religion and the Dawn of a World without Gods. Albert Williams ***

Yallop, David. 2007. *In God's Name: An Investigation into the Murder of Pope John I.* Carroll & Graf Publ. NY ***

*** Books without pagination were read on a Kindle where pages are not used

Acknowledgements

I sent a rough draft of this book to most of my siblings (7 of them) for their comments and suggestions. Not all bothered to take the time to make an in depth examination, but I appreciated those who did. My brother, Charles Joseph Odendhal III had some editorial suggestions and Margaret Creelman was the typo queen; spell checker extraordinaire. My wife, Marta Prosbova offered moral support and great cooking as she followed the progress of the book.

My friends, Annie Janus and Nasrin Rouhani and my nephew Charles Odin provided useful suggestions. Elizabeth Bishop-Martin was amazing in her critique and analysis of the grammar, typos, and had some excellent suggestions. She also wrote an essay on how to improve the book and stated that I was too critical and had to tone it down. Last but not least was Donna Gawell, the author I met on the Norwegian cruise ship Jade traveling across the Atlantic as Marta and I were on our way back to our apartment in Prague, Czech Republic. She told me about her experience in self-publishing with the help of Amazon.com. This motivated me to ignore the various rejections I had already received and stimulated me to renew my energy and determination to rearrange and complete this project. My hat is off to all of these kind souls.

About the author

Stewart Odendhal is a peripatetic world nomad who considers himself essentially a planetary citizen. He loves all animals (including humans) and plants (including weeds). His inquisitive nature forces him to learn something new every day. He is almost never bored. What makes him happy is to make humans and other animals happy. He lives with his really wonderful wife Marta Prosbova in Athens, Georgia, USA (in the winter) and in the outstandingly beautiful city of Prague, Czech Republic (in the summer). He loves to meet new people (because everybody has an interesting story to tell). He will be glad to answer any questions you may have (if possible). So go ahead and send him an email (sodendhal505@aol.com or stewartodendhal@gmail.com).

Made in the USA
San Bernardino, CA
30 October 2018